Motorcycles
on the Go

by Kerry Dinmont

LERNER PUBLICATIONS ◆ MINNEAPOLIS

Note to Educators:

Throughout this book, you'll find critical thinking questions. These can be used to engage young readers in thinking critically about the topic and in using the text and photos to do so.

Lerner Publications Company
A division of Lerner Publishing Group, Inc.
241 First Avenue North
Minneapolis, MN 55401 USA

For reading levels and more information, look up this title at www.lernerbooks.com.

Library of Congress Cataloging-in-Publication Data

Names: Dinmont, Kerry, 1982- author.
Title: Motorcycles on the go / by Kerry Dinmont.
Description: Minneapolis : Lerner Publications, [2017] | Series: Bumba books—Machines that go | Audience: Ages 4–8. | Audience: K to grade 3. | Includes bibliographical references and index.
Identifiers: LCCN 2016001049 (print) | LCCN 2016007873 (ebook) | ISBN 9781512414462 (lb : alk. paper) | ISBN 9781512414837 (pb : alk. paper) | ISBN 9781512414844 (eb pdf)
Subjects: LCSH: Motorcycles—Juvenile literature.
Classification: LCC TL440.15 .D56 2017 (print) | LCC TL440.15 (ebook) | DDC 629.227/5—dc23

LC record available at http://lccn.loc.gov/2016001049

Manufactured in the United States of America
1 – VP – 7/15/16

Expand learning beyond the printed book. Download free, complementary educational resources for this book from our website, www.lernerresource.com.

Table of
Contents

Motorcycles

Motorcycles are like bicycles.

But motorcycles have engines.

Most have two wheels.

There are many types

of motorcycles.

Riders feel the wind as they ride.

Sport bikes are the fastest. They race around tracks. Sport bike riders lean into turns.

Why do you think riders lean into turns?

Some motorcycles go off road.

This rider races off road.

How do you think these wheels help off-road motorcycles?

dirt jump

Off-road motorcycles do not

need streets.

They zip past trees.

They fly over dirt jumps.

Riders twist a handle to make a motorcycle go. Brakes by the handle and foot make it stop.

Most motorcycles carry one

or two people.

Riders wear helmets and jackets

to stay safe.

Why should riders wear helmets and jackets?

Some people ride

in groups.

They drive around town

or across the country.

Motorcycles are fast.

They are fun when you ride safely.

Parts of a Motorcycle

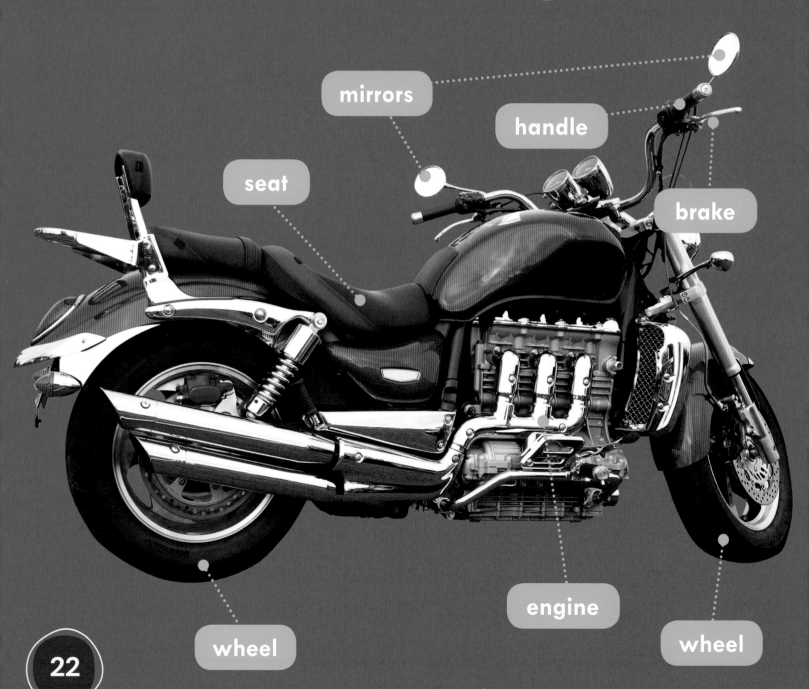

mirrors

handle

seat

brake

engine

wheel

wheel

Picture Glossary

brakes

parts that slow down
or stop a vehicle

engines

machines that
make things move

**off-road
motorcycles**

motorcycles made for
riding on rough surfaces

sport bikes

motorcycles
made for speed
and racing

Index

Read More

Bullard, Lisa. *Supercross Motorcycles*. Minneapolis: Lerner Publications, 2007.

Hill, Lee Sullivan. *Motorcycles*. Minneapolis: Lerner Publications, 2004.

Hill, Lee Sullivan. *Motorcycles on the Move*. Minneapolis: Lerner Publications, 2011.

Photo Credits